APPALACHI...

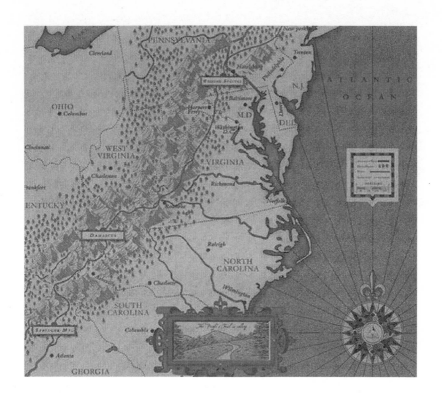

ADRIAN BLEVINS

Winner of the 2016 Wilder Series Poetry Book Prize

Two Sylvias Press

Copyright © 2018 Adrian Blevins

All rights reserved. No part of this book may be reproduced in any form without the written permission of the publisher, except for brief quotations embodied in critical articles and reviews.

Two Sylvias Press
PO Box 1524
Kingston, WA 98346
twosylviaspress@gmail.com

Cover Design: Kelli Russell Agodon
Book Design: Annette Spaulding-Convy
Cover Photo: "Smoking Section" by Martin Church (www.martin-church.com)
Author Photo Back Cover: Lisa Currie-Gurney
Author Photo Interior: Richard Smith

Created with the belief that *great writing is good for the world*, Two Sylvias Press mixes modern technology, classic style, and literary intellect with an eco-friendly heart. We draw our inspiration from the poetic literary talent of Sylvia Plath and the editorial business sense of Sylvia Beach. We are an independent press dedicated to publishing the exceptional voices of writers.

For more information about Two Sylvias Press please visit: www.twosylviaspress.com

First Edition. Created in the United States of America.

ISBN 978-0-9986314-5-5

Two Sylvias Press
www.twosylviaspress.com

Also by Adrian Blevins

Bloodline
Live from the Homesick Jamboree
The Brass Girl Brouhaha
The Man Who Went Out for Cigarettes

and, with Karen McElmurray, *Walk Till the Dogs Get Mean*,
a collection of edited essays by new and emerging Appalachian writers

Praise for *Appalachians Run Amok*

What did Dickinson say? That she knew it was poetry if she felt as if the top of her head was taken off? If that's the standard, then hell yes this is poetry, and this is poetry that has lopped off my whole head and jammed me back into where and who I'm from. Blevins has found the sweet spot, building narratives that riff, stories that sing in the voice of the most combustible, lowdown country song sung by a "punk rock of a country heart." Her subjects are Appalachian girlhood, love, death, and motherhood, in which infants smell "like not-death—like the earliest of the early yield—like kale and collards, maybe." She story-sings of places where the water is "fat with the pee foam of cattle," where people "live up a sidewinder the sidewinding likes of which only the dead can drive," where the speaker remembers herself as "a teenage fugitive in a teenage redneck's redneck truck," Frank O'Hara and Ferlinghetti in her purse, "not needlepoint," "never Einstein." Death, for Blevins, is blah, and "when I say blah I mean blah," but this poetry, cascading forward via a zillion ampersands run amok and a hilarious, provocative grief, is blah's badass antidote.

    —Diane Seuss

℘

When you're lucky enough to get your hands on a book of poems this alive, everything you say about it feels like an understatement. Yes, *Appalachians Run Amok* is utterly original, wild yet tight, feisty, vibrant, combustible. Yes, it's bursting with keen-eyed tenderness and unshushable attitude. Yes, the poems' startling emotional intelligence blends with myriad other intelligences (e.g. maternal, earthy, topical, humane, etc.) to create this voice, "all hot and giddy." A proud daughter of Appalachia, Blevins gifts us with vivid glimpses of where she came of age. Reading her beautiful, linguistically limber, cascading descriptions is like shooting the rapids with an expert river rider at the helm.

    —Amy Gerstler

℘

Wildness of spirit seems to have evaporated from American poetry of late, thinned by the turpentine of earnestness and scolding. Or maybe it all just flowed downriver into the soulful ocean named Adrian Blevins. This book has all the speed, longing, sweetness, cruelty, and sorrow of time passing (as it most surely does) through the body, anybody's body. The intelligence of the body doing the speaking here is both ferocious and generous, self-aware in the most forgiving ways—its power feeds off a deep humility in the face of the awesome daily facts. It moves me, it really does. It is also often funny as hell.

—David Rivard

&

Adrian Blevins' *Appalachians Run Amok* tells mountain secrets, but not the ones you'd think. Comical, frank, worried but not worried about it, and always in trouble, they roar up out of the gorge in swimsuits they like, letter jackets, and a fast kind of poem that can hang onto anything, including babies small as "two empty toilet paper tubes you glue together into a bazooka to blow at the cosmos through." This book is smart and wise and also lots of fun.

—Lisa Lewis

Acknowledgments

Deepest thanks to the editors who first published many of the poems in this collection, most in earlier versions and a few with different titles.

American Poetry Review: "Was Losing My Joie De Vivre Really Like," "First Elegy for the Appalachians," and "Love Poem for the Proles."
Appalachian Heritage: "Hullabaloo."
Blood Orange Review: "Love in the Blue Ridge," "Triage," and "Nothing Hurts Until."
B O D Y: "Trigger Warning."
Chattahoochee Review: "Privation Status" and "American Gothic."
Cimarron Review: "Brief Essay in the Key of 'S'."
Copper Nickel: "Pastoral."
Crazyhorse: "Status Report" and "Little Elegy."
Exit 7: A Journal of Literature & Art: "Kid Icarus," "Problem Child," and "Ars Poetica."
Florida Review: "Poem with Attitude Wearing Red Flannel" and "Appalachians Run Amok."
Georgia Review: "Tally."
Gettysburg Review: "Poem for my Mother with Frank O'Hara in It" and "Poem in Which for the Turn the "I" Impersonates Her Teenage Daughter."
Greensboro Review: "Brimstone."
Gulf Coast: "Walking It Off."
North American Review: "Explanation."
Roanoke Review: "Just Something Just There" and "Apologia."
Taos Journal of International Poetry & Art: "Meditation at the Car Lot," "Hither & Yon," and "Nine to Five."
The Baffler: "Nope."
White Whale Review: "The Plunge," "Confession," and "Testimony."
Zocolo Public Square: "The Future Was To Be Lighter" and "Fairy Tale."
Zone 3: "Memo," "This Little Catalogue of Losses," and "Bloodline."

A few of the poems in his book first appeared, in earlier versions and some with different titles, in *Bloodline*, a Hollyridge Press chapbook, Hollyridge Press, 2012.

"Tally" appeared on Poetry Daily (www.poems.com), won a Pushcart Prize, and appeared in *Pushcart Prize XXXVII Best of the Small Presses.*

"This Little Catalogue of Losses" won a *Zone 3* Poetry Award.

"Trigger Warning" was featured on *Verse Daily.*

"Poem with Attitude Wearing Red Flannel" and "Memo" were republished in *Artemis.*

"Little Elegy" and "Pastoral" were republished in Gibson Fay-LeBlanc's *Portland Press Herald's* "Deep Water: Maine Poems" column. Thanks to Gibson and the Maine Writers & Publishers Alliance.

Stuart Kestenbaum introduced "Love Poem for the Proles," "Nope," and "Love in the Blue Ridge" on "Poems from Here," Maine Public Broadcasting Network's radio show. Thanks to Stu, the Maine Public Broadcasting Network, and Maine Writers & Publishers Alliance.

Thanks to Colby College for the sabbatical that gave me the time to write or revise many of the poems in this collection and to the Humanities Division in particular for funding my visit to West Jefferson, North Carolina, where many of the Appalachians herein rest, as apparently people say, in exquisitely bucolic graves in little valleys among the even more exquisite mountains. Thanks to Tony Hoagland, Ira Sadoff, Cedric Bryant, Nate Rudy, Patrick Donnelly, Diane Seuss, Cate Marvin, my brilliant students at Colby, and many of the editors listed above for help with individual poems. Thanks to Randall Ian Wilson and Hollyridge Press for the encouragement of the publication of *Bloodline* and to Kelli Russell Agodon and Annette Spaulding-Convy of Two Sylvias Press for making this more fully-realized book possible with the ingenious idea of the Wilder Prize. Last but not least, outrageously belated thanks to Bertha Rodgers and Bright Hill Press for choosing *The Man Who Went Out for Cigarettes* for Bright Hill Press's second chapbook award in 1996, and apologies for the omission of this acknowledgement in *The Brass Girl Brouhaha.* My sincerest thanks, Bertha, for getting the ball rolling all those years ago.

Table of Contents

"What crops do they raise in this country?" the officer asked, as if he didn't much care but wanted to make some sound above the child's breathing.

"A little uv everything."

"But what is the main crop?" he insisted.

"Youngens," she said, holding the child's hands that were continually wandering toward the hole in his neck.

"Youngens for the wars and them factories."

    —Harriett Arnow, *The Dollmaker*

When asked, "What is the role of the artist in society?" Jean-Philippe Toussant replied, "To run away."

    —Suzanne Scanlon, *Her 37ʰ Year*

for Nate

and for Tony Hoagland

APPALACHIANS RUN AMOK

Swimming Hole

You can stand on the brink of the gorge and jump

      if you like your bathing suit. If the water's not too far,

           too hot, too fat with the pee foam of cattle or fish

and the soggy bodies of boys, girls, men, women

      and the Spartan elderly with their floating picnic debris

           of supple infant charges and *their* toy guns

and other bright orange pacifiers floating in the creek

      you went to in '78 sometimes for the sake of fun you guess

           or really because you were after negligence

as in to find a joint and smoke it, a beer and drink it,

      a boy to do him with a Chevy to speed in

           or a Ford to get way down and hide in

since in point of fact your bathing suit was kind of

      nasty, came from Texas or some other trash heap

           or discount barrel or psychotic middle drawer

of birthed-out cat blood and fur ruminant

      and just try to say otherwise, you nebulous little idiot,

           you long-ago fuss I think of poof I think and whoosh.

Explanation

When in doubt grow more hair

is one of the sayings I am full of.

As if a petty part of a person could be

thicker than but almost exactly like

long streams of fast water. As if

one might even get addicted to

the bodily aspects of certain sentences

and even somewhat drown in them

as though they were a bonafide

cascade. O yes a fibrous veil

of dirty blonde cells can beckon

an erstwhile child's rotten old psyche

to call to mind the rice-cracker aspects

of hair to make a kind of box

one might jump behind to be a

kitten for. I mean, to hide in

and to peek out of when the coast

is clear. O yes I admit I think this

though I am a gun-toting renegade

from algebra. And was for some time

a teenage fugitive in a teenage redneck's

redneck truck. Oh and a sad little degenerate

set loose for a day down Wild Cat Holler

in jeans ending in the too-blue

blue shape of a bell. O fuck

how the mountains would hang over us

like the wide brows on the faces of kings

while we built our fires by the creek

that was so gauzy and meek

we would walk in it sometimes

if we wanted to and always we wanted to

and so always we did: we were

the free children of Appalachia

and disliked wearing shoes

and thus would take them always off

and toss them here and there

to wander shaggy nowhere together

down that twisted stream.

Pastoral

My bravery is a daydream that comes from grass I guess

and from the first biography I ever wrote on George Washington Carver

who I chose to forever-love in the third grade

and also to persistently analyze because George was gutsy and brawny

and neurologically elastic and good at knowing about crop rotation

and at mixing things together into a nutritious mash. As a matter of fact

I did write about George in longhand in a little diary with a silver key

and though I couldn't spell any of the words like "Tuskegee"

I didn't care and neither did he because we had the mockingbirds

to keep us company and not too far away a waterfall we could climb

if we were brave enough, which of course we were. Yes that was

a slippery slope but I loved going to the falls with George

even more than I loved the slick moss and the snakes and cheese sandwiches

my mom would make with Wonder Bread since this was forever ago

and Whole Foods hadn't been incorporated yet

and was as it happens nothing but a series of woebegotten brothers

making molasses on a mountain with a mule and a Granny

who was their mother as well as a stereotype. Yes I have gone

to great lengths to explain myself by way of George to you

and still I feel provoked to continue or maybe just start all over

with my book report on Susan B. Anthony. But since that would require

feats of memory and feistiness far beyond me

I'll just assume you've had enough and wander off to the periphery

where all my people live amongst themselves

in an invisible little sachet of thirst-quenching derring-do.

Triage

Each time I fly I look a little longer out the window, so that's good, that's maybe
upgraded depth perception, but who knows since I didn't take physics

on the Smoking Block as a girl in overalls or in a Mustang at the fair
sitting cross-legged in the back with a joint or a bottle or some other joy thing

illegal, alien, licked, fringed, and laced. It was Frank O'Hara. It was D.H. Lawrence.
It was Lawrence Ferlinghetti in my purse with me trekking the sweet fodder.

It was not needlepoint. It was never Einstein. It may have been Darwin
somewhere in the back of the little skull but more likely it was condoms.

More like it was a party in the hunting shack up on the parkway where we went to fuck
because it was fucking because it was forgetting because it was rural America on drugs in
   the '70's

and not me or *about* me by any means but just another way of not dying on the spot
as in a last ditch effort or a tryout or a rabbit hutch with a ragged hole to jump swift

and brutal out of—just a country way of being urban when all we really had
was just a rope and a goat and a feral but ramshackle old heart, that sick antelope.

Appalachians Run Amok

Another thing the Appalachians don't like to talk about
is the creepy extent to which they adore the way they talk
alone in the shower & just walking around in their bandanas
versus how much they obviously meanwhile sort of also
secretly hate the high notes of their own hill-kitschy prattle,
especially if we're talking halfway psychedelic Appalachians
from mid-century America born in 1937 in Southwest Virginia,
& as it happens we *are* talking halfway psychedelic Appalachians
from mid-century America born in 1937 in Southwest Virginia
as we are talking as usual about my father who worked so hard
to assimilate & become a mutt when he traded in his wind-up radio
for certain unnamed urbanites & fake movie stars in the theatres
& bars of Richmond, Virginia, where Daddy went to college
in the '50's to be given one last chance to learn how to read
as they say & paint I guess & be a nonstop Appalachian diehard
for art. So yes in a way I do desire to keep up-to-date
on what my father gave up to become my father when he was just a boy
& pulled the monothongs out of his mouth & tossed them
in the James, but still it's hard some days for me to think of him
as in when it gives me a headache because I am not a tape recorder
or a Xerox machine or a waterway surrounding a castle
& though I'm impatient like you to get to the bottom of the problem
of what to call the vacant feeling of our long-ago deportation
from the goats & their creamy milk & the meadows & pastures
they would frolic in each Sunday when my father would

metaphorically herd them, I am not really unlike him

as in we share a DNA that likes to whisk people up & toss them

hither & yon as in long gone as in not here & out & out & away.

Fairy Tale

The Appalachians were first-rate with cigs
I think because they itched to modernize
& were biologically agitated like most settlers
& pioneers & colonists mixed in with natives
such as, on the whole, the Cherokee. But then
time passed as time in the mountains always does
if you give it time enough & the Appalachians
woke up one day wanting over & above the smokes
a little more distance between the old Grannies
& them as in the old pinto beans & cornbread
& the old garden & the old barn & up-to-date,
landmark, cig-smoking them. There were
somber brothers plowing at home & horses
& pigs to supervise as in go get the pitchfork,
let's make some hay. But we're talking newfangled
Appalachians here as in free will Appalachians
as in Appalachians in the MoMA & Appalachians
in the Uffizi in Florence, Italy, where my father
was so happy once he got there it looked like fear,
though really it was more thoroughgoing than that
as in far more cruel, for here at last was the exceptional thing
that old genius otherworldly Michelangelo had done
as in made way way way way *way* back when.

First Elegy for the Appalachians

I'd describe my forefathers the hillbillies and my Bible-thumping great Grannies
if the whole countryside in and around the mountains of Crumpler, North Carolina

weren't so sort of dead as in out-of-the-way and consequently almost empty-headed
like a spoon. As in the people who live there live up a sidewinder

the sidewinding likes of which only the dead can drive. As in a Chevron
now a percentage of the ecosystem sitting meager and dirty and silly and askance

with its pitiful little stream moving sluggish out back to nil. As in where are
the silver minnows? Where are the water moccasins and the water spiders

and the one old bridle from the 19th century horse rotted at the bottom
with only the brass mouth bit left lustrous among the rocks? There are good people

regenerating Crumpler and Grassy Creek with money from farms of Fraser Firs
and there's even a Committee for the Advancement of Art. But where's the pennyroyal

and the magic ginseng? Forgive me for being nostalgic, but where are the old timers
with their hats and rockers and ballads of privation in Wales and Ireland? Where are

the hogs gorging on chestnuts or sleeping under trees like the Devil's Walkingstick
and the Paw Paw? Naming trees is retrograde like evoking the Devil I guess

but my ancestors the hillbillies loved ghosts which they called haints just as much
as they loved whiskey which they loved just as much as they loved God

which according to my father was a blasphemous amount, so my guess is they must
lift themselves sometimes from their quaint graves and float tenacious to the New River

and in their fogginess curse us our trespasses and in their faraway fogginess
forgive us our terrible trespasses as I am talking a kindhearted people here

who I liken in general to sugar and who wouldn't ever hurt a fly,
bless their vaporous little gone-away old hearts, Amen.

Poem with Attitude Wearing Red Flannel

In other news, I'm happiest in the country going from place to place

in the early spring, looking for objects that are in my most humble opinion

not too hideous like this almost-translucent little Japanese bowl

and this not-quite pornographic sham Victorian thing. In cities I'm always

hot and restless as in kind of claustrophobic and a wee bit suicidal

as though I'm pregnant again and the emergent fetus is crushing

my vital organs again like it's the 1980's again and in order to make the owner

of a retail place just off the Lee Highway let me use the bathroom

I've got to boost my southern accent like actresses do in movies

featuring hair salons and diners because apparently filmmakers

know jackshit about southern girls except that they talk in a lilt

the filmmakers like to exploit because apparently filmmakers think

vowels sounds are sexy, which of course they are, so what I'm saying is,

being in New York or Chicago or LA is to me like having to pee

while driving on the highway in the 1980's when you're heavy with child

and have to stop at the Exxon to use what people call the facilities. But

unfortunately for you the facilities are locked, meaning now you've got

to pretend to the southern man behind the counter that you're more southern

than even his very own Mama is, saying *hon* and *bless your heart*

and *upon my word* and all like that until you're more cliché than the filmmakers

exploiting the actresses in the pigeonholing movies because that's apparently

what's required to make the fat redneck behind the counter hand over

the big key to your liberation in the nasty little bathroom where

you hope your impending child won't get syphilis or chlamydia from the fixtures

or decide to join the Tea Party once grown because if there's one thing you don't like more than a city, it's a Republican, and anyway you're actually

pretty country in actual reality in your red flannel shirt and big brown truck

going from yard sale to yard sale in the early spring singing twangy songs

to the robins and the hogs. So here in the fourteenth March of the twenty-first century

before the summer you turn 50 let's please just remember that

plus the additional and equally important bonus fact of how you're

finally sophisticated enough to end a poem by saying *fuck you! fuck you! adieu!*

to the haughty and shallow and scheming and affected in their sly white apartments

and fake feather boas, preferring evermore spring and the robins

and even the hogs heating up the old world again to a ruckus and fuss.

BRIMSTONE

Brimstone

And sex got spoiled a little too by the lady Baptists

fluttering up Main Street like a gang of fat ghouls

when they knocked on the door & almost wept

& almost said *Oh honey* out loud but shut their mouths

just in time to say it on second thought with just their eyes

in still witness against the wretched misfortune of poor me

wanting to concentrate on castaways like Gilligan

& poor me having to be the wildling child of wanton rowdies

with their drink parties & naked picture books & antiques

& paintings & ivy & other lefty vegetation not to even mention

to study witchcraft with Jeannie & Samantha on TV

with the ladies wanting me to please just study Jesus instead

as in his central predilection for eternal damnation

unless I'd repent right here, right now. The sentence is long

because the sentence means time without end, means

the sweet hereafter that is not sweet with me standing there

in my pajamas in the middle of the day like time is not nigh

but just some dreamy meadow of daises & other wildflowers

of a whole populace stripping & rubbing & licking in a swarm

like my little mountain town is a Roman bathhouse

or a novel by Henry Miller & not a perfect setting

for the Second Coming of Christ by which the ladies

are just here to kindly imply that Jesus will smote me

& smite me because that's just who Jesus is because

Jesus just wants for all these reasons & a whole lot more

to really just blow my whole sad house right down right now.

Memo

Even the large babes were small.

They were like two empty toilet paper tubes you glue together into a bazooka to blow at the
cosmos through.

They were like hummingbirds on a spit.

Hummingbirds, goldfinches, wrens—something that's got its feathers all wet in the rain out
there & the wind.

This was back when I was still so young & even more combustible—when all I wanted was
to sit on the ledge to the left there & drink a little & smoke.

That is, I was a big fretter—I had a worried brain—I couldn't stop counting what was
nineteen inches long—nineteen or twenty—like the foot plus not even the whole
calf of my little sister.

Like certain black roasting pans in my mother's pantry.

Like her dark-green throw pillows not exactly everywhere.

Like the trees behind the house that worked so hard to be tall & kill pansies.

Like the balusters of banisters spinning on the table in the cabinetmaker's shop.

Maybe that's where they'd make the elfin casket, if it came to that.

I wanted something simple & plain—pine, maybe—something with a texture of goose down
as it degraded to sawdust so the baby's littleness could be married inside that
darkness to some kind of softness like frayed wheat.

This was when I was twenty-two.

I had, as the saying goes, my whole life to look forward to.

The new little thing was giggling over there on a blanket—eyeing the world as it flitted
& sang.

The new little thing was all hot sequin & dazzle & cute pee flaunt.

Nobody was dying.

Nobody was even the slightest bit sick.

Still I sat there wedged inside myself waiting for whatever gods to come on & ruin it.

That is, as regards the serrated heaviness I seem to have to carry along inside me with its old
        edge hanging like a leaf from the top of the collarbone to a certain nervy line
        just above the pubes.

I am talking about what feeling that feels like.

What having the little ones did to me & how much each trifling half inch as they would
        grow would ache.

It is twenty-seven bobby pins in a long, bloody row.

It is a spatula.

It is a rotting harrow.

It is the plough & the rake.

It is the spade.

Testimony

My desire for the babies diminished
        after I had them, though naturally
                they were still there,

teeming like microbes in every muddy place
        I'd pick them up to ponder
                their outlandish qualities

such as they were full of angle & craving
        like those quilted squares of rice
                I used to toss in the gym

at school. Such as: water enraged them.
        And any kind of rubbing
                or sheering. Not to mention

the middle of the night with the moon up there
        being too vigorous a thing
                to sleep through. Ditto

peas from a can and corn from a can
        and anything at all
                even lightly slack,

as another snag about the babies

     was them always wanting down

          when they were up and up

when they were down. As in: they were

     foolish. And messy! And made all spoiled and knotty

          the simplest activities

such as drinking tea or walking unmindfully

     not to mention the bother

          of their constant requirements

such as rubber pants and fruit cups

     not to mention their beds and dolls

          and things to jump on and listen to

as well as the shots against diphtheria and tetanus

     and the gathering of other meds

          for the insomnia and diarrhea

making their poor mother

     in as much as destitute

          unless you consider her

always doing this song of them

     all doleful and doting

          and pining and fraught.

Hullabaloo

Things would get a little more fascinating
        when the babies got sick:

when fret would flip me open

like a latch. If the babies were hot
        I would warily

undress them. If the babies were dry

I would just as cagily but with
        my own body

feed them. And if the babies threw up

I would sponge them all over
        with a little lawless washing rag.

This is how I would get out of myself,

where in case you were wondering
        I am trapped.

Tally

The babies smelled like mixed-up milk and cotton dragged
through a little wax, but not like sugar or any amount

of caramel. Smelled like salty pee and skin swabbed slick
and the years forthcoming lit up by lemons. Smelled

like not-death—like the earliest of the early yield—like
kale and collards, maybe. Like lettuce? Smelled like

soil, though not so wholly-hearted—smelled more like
fallen apples I would say or melons rotting in baskets

made of a tincture of wheat and river water and were thus
like sleep in an antique pantry. I mean, were like sleep

that much at last. Were sleep unchained from trees
and time and fire and time and hunger and time plus time

plus longing—were sleep cut loose from up and down
and this and that and therefore were—the asinine things—

life at its most extreme and comatose and dragging and slap-
dash—yes—but thunderstruck, all the same. And yes. And best.

Confession

And then the babies began to wiggle and drop
and wander like swine on the floor of the bank

and in every you-name-it field and aisle
I guess because whatever I had or was

the ungrateful little know-it-alls
didn't want any more as in not milk and not peas

or sleep or stories and not their dad either
or any person at all upon the earth

since if you'll pardon the expression,
the babies thought that this was the shit—what-

ever *this* was—this moving on the ground so loose
and wobbly, this feeling so unfastened

and variable, this lax and spur-of-the-moment
and even slightly squalid sense

of the unchained knees corresponding to the ground
with the face and things all airy and out

unless that's wrong and I'm worse than mistaken

and we were all quite fretful and shell-shocked back then

like were all blasted up from some thunderous vault

and I'm not saying we were and I'm not saying we

weren't, but us being a family back then

may have been like us being on a little boat rocking to and fro

when it was always winter or it was worse than hot

and our skin would get stuck together ripping holes

when we'd part and I'm not saying this was my incarceration

since I was too devoted and as for my heart pounding

like a pounding wanting out, so what, so what, so what?

Ars Poetica

She was not blissful in that garden. Not
blissful harvesting it. Not blissful not.
She was not blissful not inseminated,
and couldn't stand getting vast. She
didn't like the godforsaken vaccinations:
Christ, how those children wept! She
didn't like when school was canceled,
and she liked it even less when it was
not. The very best was just before she went
to sleep, where it doesn't matter who you
are. That's when she'd lie like an old dog
in a ditch, and, yeah, she's happy saying this.

Poem in Which for the Turn the "I" Impersonates Her Teenage Daughter

As far as saying things, I say them, but what's the point.

I have read approximately every last page of David Perkins's *A History of Modern Poetry*.

I have yellow-ink-accentuated even more of it.

I have taken plentiful notes upon pallid papers in its grotesque vicinity.

I have sat upright in bed during snowstorms and admired Perkins for knowing so much
        about what I love, which is poetry, or the air around poetry that poetry agitates,
        or the poetry of the air, whichever comes first.

But, in terms of troubles, the big one is that, I, your "speaker"—your so-called speaker or
        narrator or protagonist pretending to be saying this in the present tense as you
        pretend to listen in the hypothetical future—am, biologically and therefore
        literally speaking, what is called female.

Even my daughter, who I wanted on the earth and therefore made and birthed at home
        despite a dangerously elevated blood pressure, seems to overtly hate how female
        I apparently cannot help but unfortunately be.

How old-hat make up and jewelry.

How not-literally-pink but theoretically-pink, as in the artsy earth tones of J. Jill before
        they got too frumpy.

How Tina Fay, sort of, in the Capital One commercial though not so funny.

I mean, how Late Capitalist.

How unwilling to understand that *they* the pronoun can be used to address a singular
        person in a singular body.

How increasingly wrinkly and, the weird thing is, *wrinkling*.

How *ooh la la* only historically.

Which is to say theoretically.

O how slutty, Mom, how obsolete and defunct, how sexual-of-the-hetero, how incompetent when it comes to technology and little facts about foxes such as how they dig

under the earth to find rodents to eat.

How obsessed with things being clean.

How not-exactly-astute when it comes to computers and math and except for when it

comes to poetry and this no doubt dead fellow Perkins and his clever assessments

about everything poetrywise, but isn't life more than just T.S. Eliot and the New

York School or whatever and all I'm saying, Mom, is that the planet is *dying*.

As in we are killing it.

As in like try the past tense there probably as in add that old ED as in kill*ed*, kill*ed*.

As in the planet, I say, the planet, the planet, though I will admit out of my love for you that

I am the inscrutable thing.

Each dusty cell inscrutable.

Each vowel sound when I open my mouth inscrutable.

Each black hoodie I wear, each show you like that I refuse to watch, each pomegranate I eat

inscrutable.

I love you, Mom, but I am what's unknowable and if you don't know that by now, what

do you know, I want to know.

What do you know.

LITTLE CATALOGUE OF LOSSES

Walking It Off

Whenever I try to maybe just breathe

    some appalling shit happens

        and I have to get on the couch

and pretend to recover. Even when the trouble slows

    I'm a light bulb with a skull fracture,

        a brick in a way in a dumb-dirty river

being lobbed by semi-kids in splashy shorts

    and bobby pins. And yes being tossed

        wounds the poor viscera

and no we should not be so self-important

    as to think in the plural first person

        as yes we know

we are not the protagonist of the story

    or even a semicolon

        in the middle of a sentence about it

as what really matters is America and *her* heartaches,

    her girls on rollerskates. Yes the moon landing

        and yes the GDP.

31

O Michael Jackson O Walter Cronkite O Natasha

    Richardson: what was it like

        that last second

in the US among us? Was there

    a rope to grab or was it a staircase of mist

        and did you climb to outer space

or was it more like being knocked out

    and carried into the woods

        and thrown into a ditch

or should I imagine each of you wrapped

    in receiving blankets after being

        milked and powered

or should I think up ants and other insects—

    weevils—crawling your bodies

        and what do you miss

the most? Your skin, your mouths, your

    unique way of thinking with the radio low

        and you smoking at the ravine all hot and giddy

or is it something more unspeakable

      such as your glee of the speed at which

           you rose and flew I guess

and left us so ramshackle and low-

      down and droning

         and loose?

Kid Icarus

I come from a family of rowdies who don't know their asses
some days from a hole in the ground and in this assessment

I include myself and my offspring so yes my son was drinking beer
late one night on his roof like the kids in that college town like to do

so they can mimic the stars is what I think and talk and dance
for all I know and sing. But the ladder leading up the wall

off the back deck of his apartment looked like pipes you put
water through, only less ornate and thinner. And it's warm in Virginia

a lot of the time now and in that heat like rivulets of invisible gas
and in that stupid heat like the air-flow of the chalky untellable

down the boy came like thousands of others painting their houses
and putting up Christmas lights and skiing or just walking along

The Blue Ridge Parkway and just flinging themselves over
down past the evergreens because life can be galling, a sickness,

something you might as well toss willy-nilly over a mountain
and something that can also just randomly plummet

if you inherited your mother's propensity for bare feet and the ladder
is skeletal and gaunt and the moon is pointing toward Japan

and maybe there are crickets chirping, maybe your neighbors
are cranking up the James Brown, maybe fucking and moaning, maybe

slapping, yelling, cursing the day they were ever born and *yadda yadda*
like they say on TV and *yadda yadda life has its limits* like the great poet says

and still it's all but untellable when your child falls twenty-five feet
off the top of a building and lands on the sidewalk face-down

and lives amazingly yes and becomes a so-called "walking miracle" yes I know
but that's still not the cause and effect of the whole cataclysmic tale

when there is remaining this mother sleepless when the moon
is pointing toward Japan and this mother sleepless in bed with the falling

like a racket all the time all around, the boy's ragdoll head face down,
his ragdoll legs spread out, his arms swaying like long ragdoll rags

until he's just his hat and his hat is just the green wind and he's an antique
pencil drawing, is what it gets down to: in my head all the time now

my boy is a smear of wax, a breath, a scatter of escapee powder. Oxidization.
Panic. The gasping fibers of the filaments of bird wing and dust.

Plotline

The trouble with life sometimes is how Daddy said not to be an idiot.
And up and died the winter my son fell off the roof where he'd been
spinning and whirring like he thought he was a bat I guess or a moth

spit out and spewed. So of course I stayed in the ICU and held the boy's hand—
and held and held the boy's hand—even when the call came to say
that Daddy, you know, was dead. And would be forever now

The One I Did Not Get Down On My Knees For since he'd driven to California
and seen the Pacific and trekked back home in summer boats with summer girls
whereas my son at twenty-one, where had he gone? Except into this coma

that looked like being nailed in off-key colors to the railroad track.
And into this coma that looked like rest in the sense of being a cousin to death
and this coma of the face babyish and tender except for bruising around

the crushed eye socket and the stitching they used to seal the cut they made
to put the titanium and this coma of the legs kicking and of the nurses bellowing
and pinching to get to the not-coma of waking and rising and walking and talking

on the unit where everywhere people were mashed and muddled
and crashed and jumbled in the sense of their numbers were up as in they were out of luck
whereas my son could put off being a ghost for now

since I had Daddy for that and Daddy knew what he was doing—Daddy was nothing

if not big-hearted and it would be idiotic to stay and let the boy go

so Daddy did what Daddy could and raised his hand in the classroom

and stepped off the atmosphere if that's what you call it when they up and disappear

while you're holding your breath in the ICU praying like an idiot

oh please someone get us out of this oh please someone do something and quick.

Bloodline

O, high as crazy hell and blasé like rocks was how he seemed to want to play it
there in the hospital with his hands knit loose behind his head and the one leg

lying straight across the other like he was testing a lounge chair or working on a tan
rather than becoming a flashing series of tubes and bloody wires in a bed

and comatose in point of fact in the ICU where the universe gets so mean it blathers
like a baby. Oh just hanging out and peeing off this country porch, Mom. Just pouring

a little juice into this carroty Hardees's glass on the sun-bleached Formica
the body said in its minute gestures as the nurses stripped it and eyed each other

and counted the numbers and wrote in black ink on white charts and pinched him
to try to wake him and said his name over and over to try to wake him

and called in the priests just in case and diagnosed the smell which was pneumonia
and got the technicians to cart in the machines to get some pictures and injected him

with Penicillin and Percocet and Demerol and Morphine and all the holy waters
and the holy sugars and the proteins and the very important chemical fats. But there

was something about the bloodline that I saw in my son too and came here to say
before I die—something about my own mother's faraway gaze that I could see

in the boy's shut eyes and broken jaw and my own shutdown and blacked-out old self there too in his wounded and unflappable smashed-up oblivion.

Nothing Hurts Until

you wake up concussed in Maine in the snow

without a Doberman Pinscher. & where

have all the cats gone & where the flock

of kids? & weren't they more like

ghouls & specters & / or mostly just sad

& handicapped back when you lived with them

just barely by the cow pasture in the boil

& roast if it was summer & who cares if it

was not? Who cares if you could barely

feed them? Who cares if you wrote your way

to this first snowstorm of this next winter

or talked your way is more like it & gave your art

for blankets & heaters & scarves & mittens

& a fat Kielbasa sautéed in onions with

a little fat potato on the side in a big black pot

& also so the cats could die by being injected

& not get shot in the head in the hayfield

under the black eye of the death moon & so

the kids could put on their backpacks & fill them

with notebooks & credit cards to be used at will

in the Arts Depot on campus & with one photo of you

tucked in there too of you standing by something

like dishrags & fish. Who knows why, but you want

a rifle in the picture too, & you want it rusty & gaunt

& veteran. You want tainted. You want it mean.

The title and first half of the first line of this poem are a slight adaptation from Thomas Lux's poem "Glass Eye," from *To the Left of Time*.

Problem Child

I have never written political poetry. I've just rallied against it.
I have not until this very second worn my reading glasses. And no,
I have not been hospitalized for two months or until it happened
hospitalized a child for two months or written the word *hospitalized*
three times in one sentence. It changes everything—*hospitalized,*
hospital, hospice—reiterating as it does what I, staring out the window
in the house in Maine at the end of the street on the north side of town,
now realize I was sensing back home in the heat under the tree at thirteen
as regards the lilac dying and the blackberry dying and everything alive
just one day dying and dying, to be precise. Because while the point of the oak
was to conceal me from the outlandish individuals lining up for cocktails
and pulling at their pantyhose and preparing their chins to open their mouths
for olives and pâté, there was no tree big enough to cast a shadow long enough
for me to shun the waning frogs and luckless cats and dogs and old people
and children especially wheezing inside their poorly lungs, though of course
I had to repress all this as everyone in Virginia pretended paradise
and I was told to quit my stupid huff and get inside the house
and please pour, if I would be so kind, the goddamned lemonade.

This Poem Would Be about My PTSD

if the Yankee populace colonizing the ball field of my small town

   had not gone on & stuffed themselves with more or less witch hazel

      & with somehow the many edges of a range of fabrics

as well as I think brushwood & a little pile of wine. I mean,

   just look at the lawn chairs housing the sporty Americans

      as they cheer on the not-chess players & the not-bassoonists

while bemoaning the one-sidedness of the baseball referees! So though

   I sort of want to verbalize the awful feeling like a throbbing

      or maybe like a thrumming that batters yes

& thrashes more than a smidgen & bruises in massive traces,

   these fine Americans could not care less

      about the vast insensitivities of themselves & everyone else on earth

going all the way back to before Tonya Harding

   & thus will never heed the repugnant root cellar of the big quandary here

      hotly wrong like a vehemence is what I think, & just as trembling.

This Little Catalogue of Losses

is an old burlap sack I soaked in pee & stuffed under the bed

so it could possess the fusty venom I consider crucial for the remembering of

(1) my lost youth which was my innocence & which smelled roughly of cedar & cinnamon

& (2) my optimism which was as flaxen & delicate as the wooly air above something opaque

& (3) my wildness which really was as wayward as the white flora of the mountain laurel

assailing the bootleg vicinity. & into this old sack that is in actual fact

a candid if partial register of my hitherto losses let's put (4) time too

or at least (5) some of the words for it like the *minutes* & the *hours* & the *days* & even

the *seconds*

I had then that I don't have now, though sooner or later you learn that another word for *lost*

is *gone* & that another word for *gone* is *tender* as in *knocked out* as in *grief-struck*

as in what it all adds up to, which is just a sideways forest called Hard Times

from which comes some tinny music from a high lonesome fiddle or from in my glum case

the guitar my father played before he went missing, another word for which is *died.* So

please

for my poor father's sake accept the insertion into this catalogue the real scarcity evermore of the apparatus that wasn't the steel thing people play on their laps called a Dobro

but was rather (6) something high-up & slow but spirited in Daddy's voice that people call

a twang

which is gone almost completely now from (7) my own talking like my (8) Buster Browns

are gone from my feet & (9) my clarinet is gone totally from my heart like (10) my tape

recorder

& (11) my Kingston Trio that was my father's trio really, so I shall say in conclusion

my (12) Hank as in my Williams as in (13) my grainy tape deck as in (14) my blue Toyota

as in (15) all those long & meandering back roads that got me here

with just a little something luckily leftover out of which frowzled tonight to mourn.

HITHER & YON

The Future Was To Be Lighter

And to weigh less. And to exemplify somehow
a more celestial routine

or at least not be so straight-up
old prairie weed and wind. The future

was to be wraithlike and comprise
a big craving for clairvoyance—say—

and the swiftness
of whatever's most straightforwardly

swift. There were to be more boots
and socks and hats and roots and twigs

in the future that I was to have
the vigor for and the vigor was to be

the sway which would be sort of like a wax
which was to have imbued in me

a kind of grace so that, speaking merely
spiritually of course, the universe would've

swollen up like a sponge in bubbly water

without there being an ego problem either

since I would've been made mostly

of air. Like time doesn't wear us down

to little nubs of dumb despair. Like

space doesn't. Like what we breathe

isn't Oxygen plus Helium plus Argon

plus Neon plus Methane plus Krypton

plus the confiscated wings of ladybugs

and other gremlins and woozy chemicals

the laws of poetry forbid me to name

here in the star-crossed present

where I lament the noxious resin in my lungs

since I lack the exact lingo to say

the outlook from here—the vista,

the scene—gets more

inert and woebegotten by the day

when all I wanted

was just more waggle plus

the peace I thought would come with it

like a sumptuous train or something

headed toward me like a light.

Was Losing My Joie De Vivre Really Like

regular melancholy got mad one day

& went downtown to mesh with whores

with tiny perks in their pockets

such as the already-sucked-upon wet ends

of cigs? Was it really that flat-out

low down & dumb? Or was it more like

it was too June for October

like there were tugboats on the lake

& diving boards ten feet from the shore

with kids jumping off them

with their joy still intact

only these kids weren't kids

so much as mannequins

stuffed with something buzzing in a way

like tomatoes & ferns? Was it really

winter at the time then spring

then summer then fall then winter again

around & around like a cakewalk

in the gym? Was this really the reality?

Was it the cliché? Were the bakers *really*

jailbirds dragging their most lusty confections

to imbeciles waiting deaf in running trucks?

Yes I think it was like all the gospel

had been drained out of Kentucky.

Like all the Kentucky had been drained

from Kentucky. Like all that

slow-moving fundamentalist sway

had been hacked to bits by a Viking.

& yes I was an infant in the nursery

of a new kingdom of blah. & yes

when I say *blah* I mean *blah*

which plus or minus this or that

also means death.

Brief Essay on Self-Contempt in the Key of 'S'

On the one hand, just shut up. You're a sarcophagus! Spud pheromone! Cunt-sachet!
On the other, you didn't pollute the consommé. *You* didn't erect the metropolis

or paste up that godforsaken wallpaper of megalomaniac roses
or write that sonata seeping through the pipes you didn't solder.

Then again, your mouth is a basin of smoke. Your skull is a lobster pot!
So yes you could perish and the world would go on spreading out its persnickety piss.

Yes the world without you in it would still have hibiscus exposed in books
Swathed in sensible synthetic slips: Schubert, semen, sorbet: sassafras, echo, snow.

Hither & Yon

Like you are somehow a flood. Like something too slick
in the process of being dispersed. Or like a thing let go

after being rooted for a long time beside the mountain's swaying cattails
& the six or seven pristine sycamores at the edge of things

when the mammals come to drink. Or like you are—the feeling is—
really just wind, or like the air above the forest between the full-grown

leaves of things. Or like a pair of little lungs under the rocks in the darkness
even in winter. *Especially* in winter under the rocks

is what the feeling is—like you are a you of common ice
which is like a hum or a great silence that hums,

especially when every last little thing's asleep, when
even the beavers are hiding somewhere low with their wilted branches

& shards of bark & other bunched-up underwater armaments
of time I guess & sun I guess & teeny grass I guess that's dead.

Nope

As for yes I've been against it

since ballet & I refused to leap

like a little white flag in the gym

& I refused to skate on blades

if there was ice which there was not

& I refused to ride in the backs of trucks

& did not kill my mother & father

& did not not want to either

& did not wear red bandannas

or gyrate with tassel & baton

in the Jesus parade or go door to door

with *The Old Farmer's Almanac*

or curl my hair except for that

one tawdry summer after the 7th grade

or talk with other girls about how

to fix my face or go with them

to the mall to steal bikinis there

or just lean hot against a swanky pillar

until a cowboy came by if "cowboy"

is the right word for southwest Virginia

since there were no priests back then

in the motherland. There's just lichen

now in the motherland. Just lichen

& other forms of algae in the motherland

& vines & moss in the graveyards

of the motherland whereas before

at least in Bristol there was Valleydale Foods

& hence wild gangs of handsome butchers

who'd knock on your door on Sundays

to see if you wanted some hog meat

for the freezer you didn't have in your basement

like the God you didn't have down there either

but just crickets & webs & things gone flat

like the tires on the bikes you didn't ride

& the tubes you didn't float slow

saying yes O yes down that olden river on.

American Gothic

Them high on the Dallas Cowboys
& me on Faulkner but them saying
Lynyrd Skynyrd. Their letter jackets
& bygone fields of wheat & rye.
Their love for Jesus & their doilies
on tables & their starburst quilts
& the bourbon in the cabs
of their trucks. The parkway
they liked to speed on & me high
some days on Emerson. Me high
on Woolf. Their Mamas & Daddies
& sisters & brothers. Their cousins,
their cousins. Their downy rabbits
wheezing out back. Their frothing dogs
on chains. Their vinyl recliners
& Velveeta & Farrah Fawcett posters
& pink bathrooms & venison casseroles
& fruit cakes. Me not-quite-but-almost
real high on Baudelaire. Me high
on de Sade even almost. Me high
on Rimbaud with them spitting
Skoal juice on the soggy ground
& them driving over dogs & not even
stopping to kick the corpses off the road.
Christ, it was dark. Christ, the dogs

& their pups. Christ, the foxes maybe even

& the does & fawns & possums & cats

& coons. Christ, the little lambs.

Little Elegy

Winter's no drag in Maine to me. More like
the big-fancy sister of the present tense
as in all up-to-date & forward-looking
& even vaguely avant-garde & insubordinate
like the sky itself can't say what's going to happen next
whereas back in VA the Jeffersonian troposphere
was always rusty & nostalgic like wagon wheels
& people in boots smashed at the hoedown
& despotic mothers making toy rabbits
with kids who won't leave the country store
but must lean against the sides of things forever.
Winter's back home I mean the weight & the weight
& the sad & missing vapor-mist weight-weight
of people everlastingly almost somehow passé
whereas in Maine for me at least it's not
because I'm not at all from here as in I'm not
all that much nowadays from anywhere
since by coming here I somehow left my little atoms
& proteins & other cells & whatever waters
somehow completely behind like a specter
might leave an old watch on her deathbed
& never know thereafter what the foghorn means
wailing all sopping & crestfallen like infants like that.

Poem for My Mother with Frank O'Hara in It

Ask an Appalachian to violate the law & she'll toss her pretty hose into a fetid ravine.

She will crop off her jeans.   She'll curse, she'll smoke: she will visibly amputate

the heads of   pumpkins   cabbage   crickets   fish.

Oh, she'll want to wander down the creek bed, but she'll conjugate Latin verbs instead.

She'll correct the grammar of the lady Baptists.   She will shun being sweet.

She'll eat taffy in the form of whiskey   down by the barn.

She'll get in the hay to save it from the rain.   She'll drive the tractor.

She'll shoot a baby rabbit.   She'll hear it cry,   which will be horrid.

She'll go to college & have a baby   who'll be my big sister.

She'll run away to New York.   She'll be drawn by a street artist there—

so tall   so thin   so red-headed & country.   So acute   so excessive   & fresh.

Her hair will be short,   it will be the late 1950s and

all of America   will feel like America   finally commencing,

like pink is a good color for the gist to be   like everything's up-&-coming

like shoots are poking out of the sides of buildings

flopping their foggy tongues against the past inside of everything.

& maybe Frank O'Hara sees my mother there & admires her for shunning the cows

& the accents & the cornhusk dolls & the quilts & the reapers & the rakes & the hoes

because who wouldn't?   That shit   let us admit   can be ridiculous.
But New York is loud   New York is impenetrable   like everything's a car wreck
& a tragedy   made of electricity   & pee

& there are no meadows in New York, either—   no ponds   no pastures   no sheep.
Also the horses in New York are fascists. They do what the cops say. The cops of New York,
they say go, & the horses of New York?   They go.   But in Appalachia

the wildlife has its own way of doing things. In Appalachia the horses never met a cop
they didn't want to humiliate, whereas in Appalachia the horses stop whatever they're
            doing
to amble down the creek bed looking for watercress since hunting for honeyed things

is a great way to live, as all the Appalachian horses seem just somehow to know.   You
            chew off
the rein.   You spit out the bit.   & no matter where you are after that or what anyone says
or how stormily,   you've done it,   you've made it,   you're home.

62

MEDITATION AT THE CAR LOT

Love Poem for the Proles

My unpredictability cancels out my fidelity, which cancels out

my trifling punk rock of a country heart which loves ruin

more than Easter eggs and real eggs laid by real birds in real nests

more than the female nakedness in the burnished black jacket

trying to sell me something here on the *HuffPo* where I spend all day

going from bad-news commotion to worse-news upshot

like it's my expertise to catalogue the twenty-first century's decomposition

like I went to school for that and wrote a book on that when really I'm just

lazy and domestic. Not yet a Granny in a rocker on a porch in West VA,

but, you know, little half-pink roses on smocks and a fat philodendron

in a white wire basket! I want to contradict the fluttery hankerings-after of woodpeckers

with suet and the white light of the Maine sun this one-time winter day

with maybe an umbrella that I want to buy at the Pottery Barn in Kittery

because the ads everywhere for them have evidently entered the wanton me

who's easy to dupe as another contradiction I forgot to mention is,

I am a yacht of yearning for cotton sheets. I am a cruise liner of lust

for porcelain. And inside the uterus too since there's no small human swelling

to cost me money there I count six or seven at least tiny blue bottles

for holding sad little notes marking my need for large leather bags

and a new suitcase that isn't covered in airport dirt and skinny jeans

and boots and other overt markers of my leftist good intentions such as bumper stickers to put on the suitcase saying in pithy little phrases

in especially hipster font how completely I relate

to the working stiffs jack-hammering out there right now

a new smooth street not ruined by potholes so I might get in my Honda

and drive by them and wave a wave saying they are they and I am they too

in a way thanks to my love for them. Hello Michael Johnny Catherine Isabella

and Duke! I am guilty of bad things such as I drank a gin last night

in a nice hotel that I later heard you were boycotting for better wages

so I'm writing this apologia from me and America that will not feed you to you.

Just Something Just There

I was wallowing along inadequately inside myself
just using caution on the highway like the good sign said

when a breakdown in the ambiance hurled it out there
that my pussy was the knob on a suitcase in an atrium

or a sack of potatoes or a teeny pile, perchance, of snow.
A set of cardboard boxes. A pip upon the ground.

A bonnet, a barrette, a little oval-shaped piece of soap
in a terracotta pot. Like something a rustler might

just take & lift I guess & filch & not lightening either
but just a rake or a spade & not even mine either

but just something just there like a bough or a branch
or a box of milk or a scarf on the back of a chair.

Not the heat & not the fervor. Not the ardor, People.
Not the zeal & the vehemence. Not even the aching

& not the salt. Not the swelling & not the blood,
but just a torpid flatness sitting on a table to be made off with

by whatever whomever had it the ample glow

like bars & bars of gold I guess in a noxious ditch?

Trigger Warning

There are some facts. Such as real killers & rapists.

O & the vastly ignorant waving their flags for God

while donning white hats that look like dunce caps

& bulbous men in Evangelical hair unbuckling their belts

not knowing a vagina from a fig & what a clit even is

as they sit in the slack afterword in lawn chairs

talking among themselves in opposition to breastmilk

while spewing out the real American purposes

of tits & jobs & roads & banks & saying but not saying

but still thinking & thus saying in puffed-out little

code utterances how it all belongs to them—

the women for their beds & kitchens & the jobs

for their pockets & the banks & the rivers for their dioxins

& O don't get me started on my beloved mountains

& the fracking, the cancer in the waterwells, the little

Appalachian babes making a happy racket in creeks

of coal soot & splashing around in petroleum baths

& smelling like soap & Mountain Dew

& Dow Chemicals & whatever additional crazy mix

their Mama & Daddy's on—Pabst Blue Ribbon

& McDonald's & this or that whatever homemade med.

& those who are a little better as in at least they're not

actual killers are just *a little* better—people fuck everything up

in the city & in the country in equal measure & in

different ways though mostly in the same old dumb human ways

& that's just how it is which is why I too am sick of America

of which I too sing. Meanwhile my mother said

the worst thing she ever saw was a fieldhand with a calf.

My mother doesn't knit, but for the sake of this pastoral

let's say she was knitting or quilting which she used to do

when there was some baby on the way & that she

didn't look up from her handiwork when I asked her

what I asked her. My mother gave me the truth there

when I was twelve about what she had seen when she was twelve

& it could have been far worse & yet it was not nothing

as a fieldhand with a calf is not easy for a child to see & think about

& to hear about later & to have to know about & so carry

& still I'm glad to know it & to carry it & to pass it on here

since the only thing we could do anyway was go on doing

whatever we were doing in the first place all those years ago

such as make the beds & sweep the floors & wipe the counters

down: in the rural South in the past there's domestic work everywhere

if you're me & my mom's my mom with her grin-&-bear-it

& gird-your-loins philosophies of suck it the fuck up, which I

hereby thank her for & pass also on. So what O unseeing child

do you object to the most? The rapes? The killings?

Dioxin crusting the Kanawha River in a melanoma silt

like a sprinkling of flour for a cake? The fieldhand with the calf?

The word *clit*? The *thing* clit? O you silly baby reading this

who wants to call some god or law. What god? What law?

Meditation at the Car Lot

It's anyone against the wind tonight
& each of us also against & to what avail
some sick taint in the broccoli
raining through our guts like venom. It's anyone
against MS tonight & whatever cells
fall too low in general excellence

& it's me in particular in my head tonight
against the tin onslaught of the car lot
that's really an onslaught I think against
the earthy essence where once did yummy chickens
hatch & dwell & die. Where once was the farm
of Mister McDonald & a sweet northern orchard

where once were apples plus other apples
& one could flutter down one's old Granny's
old granny quilt. & upon it lay a basket.
Hey, say me saying this is kind of like an ax
& that an ax is kind of like a warning sign
someone put on a piece of wood

all those years ago when the daft lumberjacks
began their foul felling until we got
this Nissan & this Honda & this other Nissan
& this other Honda & this GMC truck thing

& this other one & other one & other one

& other one & other one & other one

nothing like but just as grotesque as

the felled & rotted heads of horses

& the felled & rotted heads of cows & goats

& even of two or three boys & girls

who passed by here all those years ago thinking

what a good-looking paddock, what a Monet.

The first line of this poem is borrowed from Ralph Angel's "Months Later," which first appeared in *American Voice.*

Apologia

As for love I'm in favor

but how to say it is frankly

the hindrance if you were

an unfeigned monkey as a girl

or a wind-up toy monkey

or a just a honey monkey

stupid on the back of a bike.

A monkey in a school play

on monkeys! A monkey

with a monkey for a heart

watching Jane Fonda & Jane

Seymour & Jane Goodall

on TV to learn the basics

such as how to kiss & dress

& who to moon for or dupe

& ditch & block or shut in

& asphyxiate. About love

I am saying there should have been

in those mountains a Cherokee

with clichéd feathers for a hat

& a series of instructions

made of hand waves & smoke

& little hearts & arrows

drawn in the dirt meaning

touch here & here & good

& go while above the feathers

flit fairies like in Disney

& Shakespeare & fireflies

like in real life in summer

in Virginia with their heat

all over the whole situation

like love's a bang or a kiln

& not this other nighttime

repentance thing in January in Maine

so tongue-tied & faraway.

Love in the Blue Ridge

I know a lot of mountain people who'll leave home

for maybe 24 hours like they think they're obliged

like they think they signed a contract but must

return ASAP is my point to lie flat on the ground

to slowly rub the Kentucky Bluegrass & even the

Hairy Bittergrass no matter the season or temperature

or state of general heath & weep almost a little or a lot

& sigh, which is how you learn what love is

in the Blue Ridge. How tied to the earth love is,

how like it's where the chicken coop is

like love basically *depends* on the chicken coop

or just the shadow the chicken coop used to cast

now that the chicken coop has been eliminated

like the ghost of the chicken coop stains the ambiance

like love's a hurricane of feathers & beating hearts

& livers & eggs & nesting boxes & gristle & blood

flying everywhere with that fox in the spirit-coop

with us too biting us together by biting us to time

& to the air & the wind & the limestone itself

as to a grave-esque void that is not a void

so much as a bawdy richness & a tenderness

& even a roundness or a weird oneness

that is also potentially sentimental I know

but is meanwhile also a wholeness, is my point,

& a holiness. Meaning we know where home is

as in where the wholes are. Meaning how

to enter them & what they're made of & how

to dwell in that hovel & trounce it & fill it & stay.

Status Report

I love-love-*loved* the alphabet
back when I could use it to go OMG & WTF

vis-à-vis some shady late capitalist wrongdoing
such as the rich & famous floating off the continent

in the most flagrant of boats, leaving just
the youngsters & me here on the prairie

to keep everything intact with just this sugar on the mantle
in its charismatic tin. But then the youngsters

got up from the knitting circle & put down their seedcakes
& other organic whatsits, saying OMG & WTF to me

as in *in reference* to me like what I had on was not just
the dress, the feeling unfortunately was, but also

a shawl as in a cloak as in a stole as in a shroud.
That's when I finally knew what animals

youngsters just naturally are. What piles of tractor parts.
What fishheads in a sink! So now I'm using my Rosetta Stone

to examine the language of rhinos for the impenetrable skin

& the language of axes for the battle for when our foes return

to knock down our pretty little door. & here

I just wanted to sit out the rest of my days

with my sweeties by the hearth & talk the talk to hold at bay

whatever apocalyptic thing's got our number as in our address

as in the extent to which we were born to fight moneyed reprobates

with just our lingo as in our candidness & cheeky verbal fluidity

if that's what you want to call running out the clock on the ends of things

in an old lonesome song like this.

Mourning Song

I wanted to write
a feeble thing
more or less
of a song—
something
brothy & light
which if it
could be a plant
would be
more ice bark
than any-
thing. I just
wanted to say
just one thing
to befit a loon. As in
like a halted
hummingbird
to say my mourning adieu
to this forlorn &
cut-off
but matchlessly
woodsy place. But always
the head is mayhem
& a rattle gets
in. Which is just

fret & wreck. Just

death & its cape

& death & its drape

like death's

a drummer plus

some trombone

like whatever's

coming next

is going to be

one big fucking

grand parade.

Adrian Blevins is the author of *Live from the Homesick Jamboree* and *The Brass Girl Brouhaha;* the chapbooks *Bloodline* and *The Man Who Went Out for Cigarettes;* and a co-edited collection of essays, *Walk Till the Dogs Get Mean: Meditations on the Forbidden from Contemporary Appalachia.* She is the recipient of many awards and honors including a Kate Tufts Discovery Award for *The Brass Girl Brouhaha* and a Rona Jaffe Writer's Foundation Award, among many others. She teaches at Colby College in Waterville, Maine.

Publications by Two Sylvias Press:

The Daily Poet: Day-By-Day Prompts For Your Writing Practice
by Kelli Russell Agodon and Martha Silano (Print and eBook)

The Daily Poet Companion Journal (Print)

Fire On Her Tongue: An Anthology of Contemporary Women's Poetry
edited by Kelli Russell Agodon and Annette Spaulding-Convy (Print and eBook)

The Poet Tarot and Guidebook: A Deck Of Creative Exploration (Print)

Appalachians Run Amok, Winner of the 2016 Two Sylvias Press Wilder Prize
by Adrian Blevins (Print and eBook)

Killing Marias
by Claudia Castro Luna (Print and eBook)

The Ego and the Empiricist, Finalist 2016 Two Sylvias Press Chapbook Prize
by Derek Mong (Print and eBook)

The Authenticity Experiment
by Kate Carroll de Gutes (Print and eBook)

Mytheria, Finalist 2015 Two Sylvias Press Wilder Prize
by Molly Tenenbaum (Print and eBook)

Arab in Newsland, Winner of the 2016 Two Sylvias Press Chapbook Prize
by Lena Khalaf Tuffaha (Print and eBook)

The Blue Black Wet of Wood, Winner of the 2015 Two Sylvias Press Wilder Prize
by Carmen R. Gillespie (Print and eBook)

Fire Girl: Essays on India, America, and the In-Between
by Sayantani Dasgupta (Print and eBook)

Blood Song
by Michael Schmeltzer (Print and eBook)

Naming The No-Name Woman,
Winner of the 2015 Two Sylvias Press Chapbook Prize
by Jasmine An (Print and eBook)

Community Chest
by Natalie Serber (Print)

Phantom Son: A Mother's Story of Surrender
by Sharon Estill Taylor (Print and eBook)

What The Truth Tastes Like
by Martha Silano (Print and eBook)

landscape/heartbreak
by Michelle Peñaloza (Print and eBook)

Earth, Winner of the 2014 Two Sylvias Press Chapbook Prize
by Cecilia Woloch (Print and eBook)

The Cardiologist's Daughter
by Natasha Kochicheril Moni (Print and eBook)

She Returns to the Floating World
by Jeannine Hall Gailey (Print and eBook)

Hourglass Museum
by Kelli Russell Agodon (eBook)

Cloud Pharmacy
by Susan Rich (eBook)

Dear Alzheimer's: A Caregiver's Diary & Poems
by Esther Altshul Helfgott (eBook)

Listening to Mozart: Poems of Alzheimer's
by Esther Altshul Helfgott (eBook)

Crab Creek Review 30ᵗʰ Anniversary Issue featuring Northwest Poets edited by Kelli
Russell Agodon and Annette Spaulding-Convy (eBook)

Please visit Two Sylvias Press (www.twosylviaspress.com) for information on purchasing our print books, eBooks, writing tools, and for submission guidelines for our annual book prizes. Two Sylvias Press also offers editing services and manuscript consultations.

Created with the belief that great writing is good for the world.
Visit us online: www.twosylviaspress.com

The Wilder Series Book Prize

The Wilder Series Book Prize is an annual contest hosted by Two Sylvias Press. It is open to women over 50 years of age (established or emerging poets) and includes a $1000 prize, publication by Two Sylvias Press, 20 copies of the winning book, and a vintage, art nouveau pendant. Women submitting manuscripts may be poets with one or more previously published chapbooks/books or poets without any prior chapbook/book publications. The judges for the prize are Two Sylvias Press cofounders and coeditors, Kelli Russell Agodon and Annette Spaulding-Convy.

The Wilder Series Book Prize draws its inspiration from American author, Laura Ingalls Wilder, who published her first *Little House* book at age 65 and completed the last manuscript in the series at age 76. Wilder's autobiography, which she wrote in her late 60s, was published in 2014, after having been rejected in the 1930s by editors due to its "inappropriate" and "mature" material. Two Sylvias Press is proud to introduce a poetry series featuring women over age 50—young women may be wild, but mature women are *wilder.*

To learn more about submitting to the Wilder Prize, please visit:
http://twosylviaspress.com/wilder-series-poetry-book-prize.html

The Wilder Series Book Prize Winners and Finalists

2016:
Adrian Blevins, *Appalachians Run Amok* (Winner)

2015:
Carmen R. Gillespie, *The Blue Black Wet of Wood* (Winner)
Molly Tenenbaum, *Mytheria* (Finalist)

69114752R00066

Made in the USA
San Bernardino, CA
12 February 2018